PUBLIC SPEAKING FOR TEENS

How to Write a Speech,
Learn to Debate, Speak With
Confidence, and Overcome
Your Fears!

Jamie Myers

ISBN: 978-1-957590-33-2

For questions, email: Support@AwesomeReads.org

Please consider writing a review!

Just visit: AwesomeReads.org/review

Johnson

FREE BONUS

SCAN TO GET OUR NEXT
BOOK FOR FREE!

Johnson

TABLE OF CONTENTS

CHAPTER ONE:

WHAT IS PUBLIC SPEAKING

We've all heard about public speaking. Most of us have had to do it too. Public speaking is a vital, pivotal part of the school experience. There's hardly a student around who hasn't had to give a speech about something as they progressed from kindergarten to high school.

You've probably seen people give speeches on various topics. Maybe it was about the life of Abraham Lincoln, how to groom a dog, or the story of their favorite summer vacation. There are many different subjects that someone can give a speech about. But no matter the matter at hand, the basic idea behind any public speaking is the same.

Public speaking is hard for a lot of people, especially young students. As teenagers, you might be going through a complicated, confusing, and sometimes challenging period of life. Public speaking just adds extra anxiety, which can make many people feel self-conscious, afraid, worried, and sometimes frozen with fear.

However, it doesn't have to be that way! Public speaking is nothing to be afraid about, not if you really know what you're doing and understand your topic. By following some simple tricks of the trade and a few rules, you'll no longer have to be afraid of it.

In fact, you'll soon see all the benefits public speaking can bring you and understand that it can make you a better student, researcher, and overall communicator. But you'll also find out that giving public speeches can make you more confident in every area of life. Public speaking is nothing to fear. Instead, it's something to embrace and ultimately enjoy.

THE BASICS OF
PUBLIC SPEAKING

Public speaking is almost like a performance in front of a live audience. Public speeches often touch on a wide range of subjects. The objective may be to inform, amuse, or persuade the audience. To support the discourse, visual aids may include electronic presentations, which listeners find more engaging.

A public speech usually has a time and venue restriction. PowerPoint slideshows are often used online, or they employ a speaker's prerecorded footage. This also applies to live recordings of public speaking performances.

Public speaking has occurred for centuries. However, most public speaking professionals who work in commercial communications date the history of contemporary public speaking to ancient Greece and Rome.

Of course, there were no slide displays in previous civilizations to facilitate public speaking. However, live performances were commonplace, and public speaking techniques were developed that are still in use today.

The primary purpose of public speaking in ancient Greece was to flatter or influence listeners. Greek citizens once had the ability to propose or object to laws during assemblies, which required public speaking. The art evolved into a skill that was taught and practiced. *Rhetoric* was the term used by the Greeks to describe public speech.

When Rome rose to power, public speaking was common in senate sessions that employed rhetorical techniques borrowed from the Greeks. The majority of public speaking instructors at that time were Greek.

Up until the middle of the 20th century, the Latin method of public speaking was widely used in the U.S. and Europe. A much less professional and more casual speaking style gained popularity after World War II. Additionally, electronic tools for enhancing public presentations became accessible. These electrical gadgets were computerized around the end of the 20th century. One of the tools that we're familiar with and utilize today is PowerPoint.

Most people will tell you they dislike public speaking. Given that speaking in front of groups is a frequently mentioned fear, many people admit to being terrified and trying to avoid public speaking to large groups of people. If this is you, you're missing out on acquiring an important and entertaining skill.

There are many kinds of speeches. A lot of people need to give speeches for weddings or other family events. You've surely seen someone give a toast in front of people at a family event. Well, that's a form of public speaking. Or maybe you're trying to get a job and ace a job interview. Whether you know it or not, that's public speaking.

Of course, many students give speeches as assignments in school. From history class to English and beyond, there are many class assignments that require making a speech in front of your peers. And the truth is that it's not easy. Even if you know your material and you've done your research, public speaking can still be frightening, especially as an inexperienced student.

You'd think it would be easier since crafting a speech isn't all that hard. The structure of a speech is fairly simple: first an introduction, then the statement you intend to make, then the reasons that support your statement via evidence, facts, research, and more. Of course, every speech should end with a strong closing statement. Pepper your speech with personal anecdotes, stories, and beliefs; there's a lot of room for improvisation and fine tuning, but the basic premise behind your speech will be the same. Creating and performing a speech is easier if you stick to a standard format.

If you can get your mind around the idea of public speaking and practice away your fear, you'll see that public speaking presents great benefits that go way beyond just getting a good grade.

HOW PUBLIC SPEAKING BENEFITS YOU

Public speaking as a communication skill has become increasingly important in business, government, and education in recent years. Your speech can be informational, persuasive, edifying, or even entertaining, and in the hands of a prepared speaker, the spoken word may be more potent and convincing than the written one.

Whether you're a student who has given many speeches in your life or you're practicing for your first one, you'll benefit from honing your public speaking abilities. The following are some advantages of skilled public speaking:

- More confidence
- Improved research ability
- Enhanced deduction skills
- Becoming a better all-around student

But here's another thing public speaking can do for you: It can greatly improve your social skills. This makes perfect sense when you think about it — social skills are about communicating. A major part of education is being comfortable interacting with others, talking to people you don't know well, and feeling at ease just being yourself. Those are all things that don't come easily for everyone, but with practice and experience, they might. Public speaking is like any other skill you've learned—the more you do it, the easier it becomes, and pretty soon you don't give it a second thought.

You now recognize the advantages of public speaking. You may have a little more passion for the subject, or you may still believe it's not for you. Perhaps you've never delivered a speech that was well received or public speaking still terrifies you. The important thing to remember is that public speaking is a skill that anyone can learn. All it takes is a little hard work and practice.

WHY YOU MAY BE SCARED OF PUBLIC SPEAKING

There are people who don't have a problem with public speaking. Maybe you don't feel anything but ease and excitement when you get the chance to give a public speech. That would be great news indeed.

Sadly, many others aren't like that. A lot of people get nervous or scared when they hear that they'll have to give a speech. Did you know that there is an official name for the intense fear of social situations like public speaking? Experts call it *glossophobia*, a social phobia that people feel when they have to perform.

Surprisingly, most people who have glossophobia don't show symptoms of other types of social phobia. Therefore, you might be completely comfortable meeting new people or performing tasks in front of others. Yet, you still feel petrified when told to give a speech to an audience.

If you're really afraid of public speaking, you might have difficulty breathing, begin to sweat, or feel your heartbeat speed up. These are distinctly unpleasant reactions to the anticipation of speaking in public.

But it can be worse than that. There are complications that can result from an unusually intense fear of public speaking. Studies have shown that people with social phobias have a higher-than-normal risk of developing anxiety or depression. This is usually because they feel isolated and alone in their fear of public speaking.

Maybe the reason you don't like public speaking is hard to figure out. Maybe you don't even know why you're so afraid of talking in public, but you know the fear is hard to avoid and overwhelming.

At the end of the day, it doesn't matter *why* you don't like talking in public. Whatever the cause, it's possible to overcome it and successfully give a public speech in a different way that feels comfortable, right, and doesn't cause you to break out in a cold sweat the moment it begins.

HOW TO WRITE A SPEECH

You've undoubtedly endured some less-than-stellar speeches. These speakers didn't understand the value of your time and missed the point that your attention was entirely voluntary as well.

When you write a speech, you want to make a positive impression and leave your audience with one or two takeaways they'll remember. The rest is purely fun. How do you convey those important points?

STAND OUT

This one seems simple in principle. Of course, pulling it off requires discipline and creativity. First and foremost, remember that an audience frequently retains only one line of what you said, so it's important to make yourself and your speech stand out.

Other rhetorical strategies can also make an impact. Major public figures and politicians use intense memorable pictures that suggest strong emotions and feelings associated with patriotism and the potential of people and country. Speakers might flout audience expectations to be noticed, however. Maybe they say something controversial or unexpected, something that shakes things up and fixes attention directly on the speaker. That's a smart approach, too, because it makes an unexpected impact.

ESTABLISH
A STRUCTURE

Think back to a disastrous speech you once heard. What made you lose interest? The speaker most likely deviated from a reasonable course.

A good speaker should provide both a road and a destination for the audience. They're curious about your destination and motivation, so make it clear at the outset what you're going to discuss. Focus on organization and simplification when you write and edit your talk. Eliminate everything superfluous, conflicting, or unclear. Keep in mind that if it doesn't help you communicate your main point, reassess or drop it.

DON'T WASTE
THE OPENING

Speakers too often waste their openings when their listeners are most attentive. Come out strong when you write. Give a startling statistic or key information. Share a funny story that relates to your big idea. Use a question as an opener and ask the audience for a show of hands. Engage your audience from the beginning, and keep your address interesting and lively. If you don't, your listeners' attention will wane, and they may leave or mentally check out. Take advantage of the momentum you have when you first get up on stage.

FIND YOUR VOICE

Who is your audience, and what brings them out to hear what you have to say? Before you start writing, know the answers to those questions. Whether you're crafting a speech to enlighten, inspire, amuse, or even challenge, always live up to the expectations of your audience. Using the right tone sets you off on the right foot.

Study your message. Does it adhere to the spirit of the occasion? Will it inspire people to be their best? Here's some guidance when you speak in a formal situation: Concentrate on being positive and inspiring. Remember that people may forget facts and figures, but they won't forget how your speech made them feel. If your audience shows appreciation and enthusiasm at the end of your talk, consider your speech a success. That in itself is a message, and they will share it with others.

HUMANIZE YOURSELF

You and your message are inseparable. If your target audience doesn't believe in you, they may reject your message. It's that simple. Your speech and body language make the strongest impression. However, there are certain methods to connect through language.

Make a joke about feeling nervous; all the other students listening to you can relate to that feeling. Include family references and other information that you know firsthand. Write as though you're chatting with a good buddy. You're not trying to sell or preach; just be who you are. Be your most authentic self onstage.

REITERATE YOURSELF

Repetition is the secret to creating effective speeches. Drive home important terms, ideas, and concepts to help listeners remember what you said. Always search for ways to reinforce points in a way people can relate to.

Repetition could irritate some of your listeners. Don't be overly concerned about that; your goal is for people to remember your content six months from now.

BE BRIEF

What is the most serious public speaking sin? The answer is attempting to cram too much information into your presentation. After a while, the attention span of your audience inevitably diminishes. So, state your case with all the essential information, thank the audience for their attention, and then take a seat. Remember: This is not your time; it's their time.

CHAPTER TWO:

PRACTICE PUBLIC SPEAKING

If you have a speech or presentation coming up, friends and family make excellent practice audiences. Invite them to listen to your speech and provide you with honest feedback. (Honest feedback is invaluable; evaluate it objectively.)

The fact that they know you is the significant advantage of presenting to family members. Since they know you well, they can tell if you sound natural or come across as inauthentic. They can also alert you if something seems off. You'll feel more at ease speaking in front of your bona fide audience if you've rehearsed in front of family or friends you trust and received feedback from them.

What is the best approach to having family watch and critique your speech? Well, it's not as easy as asking them to watch you give your presentation.

You need to shake it up a bit more than that. Let them choose a topic for you. That's right; don't just do a practice run of the speech you're giving to class. If you really want to have your speaking skills examined, critiqued, and perfected, give a speech you haven't practiced.

You don't have to get all the facts right when you present to your family. It's more about how you feel in front of an audience and how you perform. The family members watching won't judge you based on facts or accuracy but rather on how your personality comes across and how engaging you are. You know you'll get the facts right when you're giving your speech; your family members will be watching the performative aspects of your speech.

Your family and friends love you, so they might feel a tad uncomfortable telling you the unflinching truth about your stage presence. Imagine giving a poor presentation when you obviously have a lot of room for improvement. Your family members may feel uncomfortable telling you; they might hold back on critiques that could make your speech much better.

That's why you have to tell them to be brutally honest with you. Ask them not to hold back. You want the ultimate, honest, utter truth above everything else. It will be the best feedback you could possibly get. In fact, it's invaluable!

PRACTICE
WITH FRIENDS

Practice in front of your friends as well as your family. In fact, it's even smarter to practice *with* your friends.

How exactly does that work? Well, you can get together with other people in your class. You can help classmates with their speeches, and they will be more interested in being honest and truthful with you in return.

Your friends and classmates who will also give public speeches can give you helpful, focused advice about your presentation. They can tell you if you're veering off topic, if your speech doesn't make sense, or if it's missing something. They know the assignment better than your family, so in many ways, they're an ideal audience to hear you practice your speech.

When you practice in front of your family, you're reciting a speech that isn't the one you'll give in class. But when it comes to presenting in front of your friends, you *do* want to give your actual speech. Your friends will understand the assignment and know what the teacher expects. There is no one better to tell you what needs to be tweaked, improved, or removed.

Be sure you offer something to friends in return for their help. For example, make it a fun night with pizza and snacks. Have fun while you rehearse your speech and get feedback. It's also important to offer feedback to friends after hearing *their* speeches, just like they listened to yours. Return the favor because they helped you. Also, when you listen to their speeches, you might think of ways to improve your own; it's a win-win situation for everyone.

REVIEW OTHERS

Consider the speakers who have inspired or motivated you. Those speakers put a lot of labor into their speeches, which helped you remember them. Perhaps it was the way they talked, the accessories they employed, or the slideshow that played in the background. To be genuinely outstanding at public speaking, you must be able to control many factors. Fortunately, there are many public speakers available to study and emulate.

You must choose your favorite public speaking style. When selecting speakers whose styles you admire, there are a few important considerations to keep in mind. First and foremost, look for speakers who share your values. They will not be talking about what you're speaking about for your class, but they must share your style of communication. When you succeed as a public speaker, keep in mind that you're hunting for speakers who are similar to the ones you admire. While they are not required to be exactly like you, they also shouldn't be totally different.

Take pains to find someone who, in addition to personality and fundamental beliefs, reflects the style you're happy with. Avoid listening to presenters who use a lot of acting or impressions in their presentations if you're not comfortable with either. You ought to be able to see a speaker and think *I could do that* when you observe their gestures or body language.

RECORD YOURSELF AND WATCH

Videotape your speeches and presentations whenever you can. By watching and listening, you can analyze your performance and figure out what you need to change.

It might be challenging to get over the uneasiness of watching yourself on camera. Concentrate your analysis on key areas to give you good feedback. Watch the video a few times to get a solid sense of any changes you want to make.

Keep track of any uncomfortable pauses or how often you say involuntary crutch words such as "um" and "like." Look at your posture and mannerisms. Do you look comfortable or stiff? Do you look directly at the audience? Do you smile? Is your voice clear throughout the speech?

Keep your motions in mind. If they seem forced, work on a relaxed posture and easy stance. Make sure everyone can see what you're doing, especially if you're standing behind the podium.

Finally, consider how to handle interruptions such as coughing or a question you weren't prepared for. Practice handling interruptions like this with a smooth reaction so that you improve even more the next time it happens.

If everything went well, you might utilize the tapes as part of a marketing effort to advertise your public speaking services, including your demo videos.

Keep a copy of your tapes to keep learning from your recorded speeches and presentations. Before the speech, find out if it will be taped so you're not caught off guard.

The videographer may provide a duplicate DVD of your speech. Since the source recording is compressed during the DVD manufacturing process, this format doesn't work well for editing. You can make the file smaller so that it will fit on a prepared DVD and distribute more quickly and easily.

Are there other options? You can ask the videographer to obtain the raw video and simply drag and drop the recordings onto a thumb drive or external hard drive. Check to see if the data is compressed. If so, be aware that this will result in higher voice video quality than a compressed and prepared DVD.

Another problem with speeches on a DVD is PowerPoint presentations. Most people criticize the irregular slides that appear throughout the recording. After you recorded or filmed your speech, the PowerPoint was likely edited into the speech video. Editing your intended message or content to fit the slides might be challenging. Another reason why high-quality, uncompressed raw film files are crucial is that it's easier to insert slides later.

Allow other people to assist you. Always have a few thumb drives on hand so that the videographer and producers can format the data to the appropriate MAC or PC format. And always make it clear if you plan to pay to have the thumb drives shipped to you or if you plan to pick them up. Your time and work will be well spent.

Watching and rewatching recordings of your speeches and presentations may feel awkward at first, but it's a tried-and-true method for improving your techniques. Athletes, dancers, and other entertainers frequently watch videos of their performances. Analyzing recordings of your presentations is a crucial step in improving as a public speaker, from making sure you acquire the correct video to understanding what to look for on the tape.

CHAPTER THREE:

GETTING OVER STAGE FRIGHT

Many people experience stage fright, especially when they're about to give a big speech in front of a class. There is nothing wrong with that; it happens to millions of students all over the world.

But the truth is that there is a way to overcome stage fright. It requires some research, practice, and work, but it can really do the trick and make the idea of public speaking a lot less scary than it once was.

Even if you feel you don't suffer from stage fright, and the idea of public speaking isn't scary to you, you should still try to follow these procedures to see how they make you feel. You may be surprised to find that public speaking is even *easier* when you follow these steps.

DEEP BREATHING
EXERCISES

Have you ever taken a yoga class or heard about relaxation techniques to calm the mind and body before a major event? If you haven't, you should try them since these can be key methods of getting rid of stage fright. They'll help you feel ready and maybe even *eager* to give a public speech.

From sports stars to famous actors, politicians to world-renowned business leaders, breathing exercises have been used by many successful people to take away the performance anxiety that can come with public speaking. This is a terrific way to center yourself, calm your heart rate, and give yourself a boost of confidence when you need it most.

If you've ever been to a yoga class, you have likely heard about the power of slow, careful breathing. Yoga students are taught the traditional technique of mindful breathing. By training patients to concentrate just on breathing in and out, behavioral therapists can help them feel less anxious.

To perform your best in a variety of activities, including weightlifting, martial arts, opera, and stage acting, adequate breathing is essential. Although though you probably know that already, it's still important to consider. When did you last pay attention to your breathing before speaking in front of a crowd?

Most people almost certainly spend more time worrying about their clothing choices than their breathing patterns. It seems to make sense to put breathing on automatic mode since it frees up your mind to concentrate on numerous other decisions you make every day. However, failing to pay attention to your breathing can have a significant negative effect on your physical and emotional readiness.

Deep breathing can lessen tension. Although the optimal pace is closer to five breaths per minute, the average adult's respiratory rate is anywhere between 12 and 18 breaths. Most professionals advise using coherent breathing, which consists of equal-length inhalations and exhalations. Here's another way to do things differently:

- Sit up straight in a rigid chair and relax your muscles. For six seconds, inhale slowly and softly through your nose.

- As you breathe in, your abdomen should enlarge. Put your hand on your stomach, and feel it rising and falling as you practice this technique.

- Exhale softly and gently through your nose for six seconds. Feel the air as it leaves your stomach.

- For 15 to 20 minutes, continue breathing in this manner. Start with counting for two seconds while breathing and exhaling, then increase to three seconds, and then all the way to five seconds.

There are countless other deep breathing techniques you can use. Look for breathing exercises, breathing techniques, or belly breathing to get a variety of options with video instructions. Breathing exercises may be done while standing, sitting, or lying down.

Some exercises encourage gradual breathing over deep breathing or lengthier exhales than inhales. Despite the abundance of choices, virtually all of them emphasize deeper, slower breathing.

Try out several exercises, and then routinely practice your favorite to get accustomed and comfortable with it. Practice multiple times on the speaking day, including just before your presentation. Your body will be aware of your silent breathing practice as you go toward center stage, but the folks sitting around you won't be.

Breathing exercises promote calmness and focus. When you're focused and tuned in, you will perform better and get your point across better as well. All in all, your speech will be easier to give and better received when you practice serious, time-tested breathing techniques. They're a wonderful way to put yourself in the right state of mind to nail your assignment and deliver a speech that will be remembered as impactful.

VISUALIZATION TECHNIQUES

Not just for bowling, baseball, or various sports, mental images can help you perform better. They have proven to be effective for public speaking and any type of real-time performance.

Set aside time to mentally rehearse the piece you'll deliver, as well as mentally practicing it by visualizing yourself performing the speech and touching upon all the important ideas and research. Your performance will be much enhanced if you engage in accurate, multisensory, first-person imagery ending with you giving your successful speech.

It has been demonstrated that imagery is helpful in contexts other than just visual motor activity. It's normal to feel a bit anxious before giving a speech. To get over your worry or anxiety, try to visualize yourself in great detail making your speech. View it from the audience's point of view; see them as you expect to see them on the day of your presentation.

Imagine everything about the event in a multisensory way, including the sound of the audience, the room's full spectrum of color, and the feel of the mic in your hand. To make your cognitive picture as realistic as possible, take a glance around the room before giving the speech. Visualize the speech, and consider the specifics of what you'll say and how you'll say it before speaking.

Finally, and this is crucial for overcoming nervousness, see the speech flowing smoothly. Visualize yourself saying the words perfectly. Imagine a round of applause at the end, and picture the great compliments you'll receive for a job well done.

The method of treating performance anxiety through imaging is similar to the way many other anxieties are handled. You'll likely be able to use what you learned about remaining calm when the time comes.

Whatever it is you'd like to get better at, imagery offers an effective approach to do it. It's beneficial to review these aspects of your performance that you want to strategically change. These ideas often occur at a conscious, thoughtful level. It's crucial to imagine carrying out such ideas once you've decided on them.

You may create links between your strategic thinking and the areas of your brain that carry out action by thinking in the first person and visualizing an excellent performance. You get closer to realizing your objective if you see it playing out perfectly.

PHYSICAL ACTIVITY

You can have heightened tension and anxiety just before a speech or presentation. Even the greatest and most talented speakers experience this occasionally, if not regularly. Doing light physical and mental activities, also known as loosening up, is one approach to decompress and become more focused. This post will discuss a few practical physical exercises you can do to alleviate tension and lower anxiety before giving a speech or making a presentation.

Breathing and stretching exercises are perfect for both newcomers and seasoned public presenters. They are also effective in easing tight muscles, boosting blood flow, and enhancing your sense of calm and concentration.

The diaphragm is a muscle located immediately below the lungs; it contracts and expands during diaphragmatic breathing (also known as belly breathing). This is an excellent relaxation method since it calls for slow, deliberate breathing, which helps to regulate the diaphragm. Use this method in conjunction with the mental/psychological workout in the next section for best results.

How about some shoulder and neck rolls? Exercises that reduce upper-body tightness and stress include this easy maneuver. Pain and discomfort in the upper neck and lower back can result from stress and worry. When the trapezius and levator scapulae muscles are tight, you may feel uncomfortable and irritated, especially when you're standing like you would during a speech. Neck and shoulder rolls concentrate on rotating the head and shoulders to stretch and relax these muscles.

Your biceps, wrists, and several arm muscles become less rigid as you stretch them. These tissues can significantly impact your mood and comfort when speaking, as they are frequently used in a presentation. Extending those muscles can help you feel more relaxed, experience less arm fatigue, and have more range in your body language.

Waist turns are another exercise that may help you feel loose, comfortable, and ready to give your speech. This workout targets the lower back and abdominal muscles. These muscle groups make a sizable impact on your personal comfort. Waist twists may be done a few different ways, but a common one is to place your hands on your hips and rotate your waist in a circle.

The backbone of your body is made up of your upper body and core. Lateral stretches release virtually all your upper body muscles and get your blood flowing. Perform lateral stretches by tapping your toes while holding your legs together with your knees straight.

OTHER TRICKS
OF THE TRADE

STUDY HARD

Being prepared is the best way to halt stage fright in its tracks. Understand your subject matter and, more significantly, your audience. You won't feel anxious if you confidently understand your subject matter. Additionally, you won't be fazed if a technical problem arises because you already know what you intend to say.

PRACTICE AT LEAST ONCE A DAY

Knowing your material is helpful, but it doesn't always solve the issue. Rehearse as often as possible prior to your presentation.

Know your material inside and out, and rehearse as often as you can to boost your confidence. You may feel there's such a thing as practicing too much, but that isn't true. In fact, the more you practice, the better you'll know your speech and the easier it'll be to deliver when the big day comes.

GIVE YOURSELF A PEP TALK

Understand that despite being "all in your mind," stage fright may emerge physically. The greatest defense is to shut down negative talk. Don't be concerned about forgetting the material, and don't worry about all the little things that pop into your mind. They're exactly that: just in your mind. You may need to talk yourself down, but you have the power to reel in negative thoughts. Instead of being your own worst critic, be your biggest cheerleader.

Change that troublesome, nagging worry to a question. Ask yourself, "What if I'm really good at this?" A positive mindset will go a long way toward lowering your stage anxiety, even though that may sound overly simple.

Occasionally you need to slow down, look in the mirror, and say, "I've got this." Because you do. You can be your own worst enemy, but you can also be your biggest supporter.

WALLOW JUST A LITTLE BIT

Positive self-talk may help you relax, but if it doesn't, it might be time to consider the worst-case scenario. When you do this, you'll see that even the worst-case situation isn't that horrible. Your anxiety could even decrease as a result.

Don't let yourself get too carried away with this step, however. Give yourself a few minutes to think about the worst-case scenario, and then pick yourself up, move forward, and remind yourself that the worst-case scenario is quite unlikely.

FOCUS ON FIVE MINUTES AT A TIME

Pretend that your entire speech will last just five minutes. It will be less stressful as a result. Just focus on getting past the first five minutes; after that, the rest will be easy.

If your speech is going to be longer than five minutes, that's okay too. In that case, focus on five-minute increments. Focus on the opening five minutes to get things moving, then the next five minutes, and so on. Compartmentalize the speech into sections, and narrow your scope to one section at a time. This will make it easier to remember your material while staying calm and comfortable.

DON'T APOLOGIZE FOR NERVES

Most of the time, nobody will notice that you're anxious. Why tell them? Even though you may be nervous, your viewers might not notice, so don't bring it up.

You're telling the audience what to think of you and your speech by the way you hold yourself and the confidence you display. If you're nervous, they will pick up on it. Don't apologize for your nerves, and don't acknowledge them either. Remember: You've got this.

KEEP YOUR MISTAKES TO YOURSELF

You're confident in your presentation since you prepared and rehearsed it. What if you suddenly realize you have the themes in the wrong sequence or forget a crucial detail on stage? Remember that you're probably the only one who notices. There's no point in calling attention to a mistake that others weren't even aware of. If you bring it up, some people will look for additional mistakes, which could take attention away from the main point of your presentation.

BREATHE AND STRETCH

Short, rapid breathing is a tell-tale sign of nervousness; it can throw you off balance if you ignore it. Take a few calm, deep breaths before you take the stage to help you feel calmer.

You may feel tense and rigid if you're anxious. Do some stretching 15 minutes before beginning your speech. This will calm your body and ease your stiff muscles.

DOUBLE-CHECK EVERYTHING

Verify that everything is functional, in order, and ready to go for the big day. It's too late if you discover that you overlooked your materials just as you're about to take the stage. Your anxieties will undoubtedly take control. If this happens, you should be so familiar with your presentation or speech that you can carry on without incident.

WORK WITH STAGE FRIGHT

Be prepared for and accept the reality that you'll have anxiety, particularly in the opening moments of your presentation. This will work against you the more you fight it. Keeping your attention on your presentation will gradually reduce your fear.

Yes, you can work with stage fright instead of pushing back against it. Understand that it's coming, and utilize its energy to your benefit. The nervous energy and anxiety you feel can be converted into something helpful.

Talented performers will tell you that anxiety, nervousness, and excitement are very similar to each another. You can convince yourself that the nerves you feel are anticipation and excitement. Once you do that, you will likely speak confidently.

CHAPTER FOUR:

HOW TO ENJOY PUBLIC SPEAKING

Let's face it: Public speaking is something you'll do in life more than you realize. There will be times you'll need to use those skills again. You may have to give a toast at a family wedding or introduce a guest speaker at a business meeting.

In business, in your personal life, or any other aspect of living, public speaking will come into play. That's great news if you enjoy performing in front of others. But what if you still get a cold shiver down your spine at the thought? In that case, you better be prepared to make public speaking easier because most people can't avoid it forever.

If you want to get better at public speaking and really enjoy it, there are many options for you. You can turn it into something you do with ease and enjoy.

Many people find public speaking rewarding. You can find ways to get comfortable with it, and yes, even love it.

JOIN OR CREATE A CLUB

There are many different clubs that teach people how to master public speaking. In fact, there are many clubs waiting for you to join to perfect your speaking and social skills while also learning to achieve important life goals.

When most people think about clubs that help them with public speaking, they typically think about forensics. While that *is* certainly an option to improve public speaking, there are many other choices. Many clubs such as Toastmasters not only teach you to speak like a pro, but there's also an important social aspect where members make lifelong friends while taming their fear of public speaking.

There are clubs about vacationing, social skills, movies and music, and a whole bunch of other hobbies and interests. These organizations give you plenty of opportunities to chat, interact, and get comfortable speaking to others about specific topics. This is a huge step toward making public speaking easy to do. In these clubs, you might talk about a poet you love, a movie you enjoy, or your favorite musical genre. Whatever the topic, you will have to speak up and present your thoughts in a coherent, engaging way. You might not think about it at the moment, but all this "conversation" is making you a better public speaker.

How do you find a club that's right for you? If you're still in school, you have plenty of options. Check out the clubs at your school, and decide if one feels right for you. It might be the one featuring local business leaders or the one whose members are Star Wars geeks. Whatever it is, sign up and start attending meetings.

One of the clubs all schools likely have is drama club, a great place to perfect your speaking skills—one that involves the stage and live performances.

GETTING INTO THEATER

One of the best ways to improve public speaking is to recognize and embrace the fact that it's a type of performing, like reading from a script and acting in a play. Drama and theater arts are great ways to get better at public speaking and become more comfortable up in front of people.

If you're the type of person who really feels uncomfortable doing public speaking, then theater is the place for you. It will help you feel better about being in front of other people and "performing." It also allows you to better judge your performance and how much progress you're making. You will be able to see the work of others, figure out what you like and don't like, and learn how make it work for you.

If you *like* doing public speaking, then theater will help you in several ways. It will make your speech flow better and feel smoother. This will be easier on your nerves and turn an interest like drama into a rewarding experience on multiple levels.

Additionally, local theater could turn you on to a new hobby that you'll love forever. If you've enjoyed public speaking so far, you may love theater and find that acting is second nature to you. You never know; you may have found a new career idea all because you wanted to enhance your public speaking skills.

While you may thrive in theater, don't expect Hollywood fame and fortune in a few short months. Some actors who go on to become professionals start by doing plays in school shows to get their feet wet. For others, acting is never more than a hobby, which is wonderful as long as they enjoy it and find it rewarding. Be grateful, and always remember how much you gain from acting, where you learn to be a better performer while enhancing social skills and becoming a more rounded person.

Taking every chance to perform locally is a good way to start in theatrical acting, which will banish your fears about public speaking forever. Many amateur and community theater organizations offer open casting calls for upcoming plays, and actors of all ages may be needed. Most of the time, local media and word of mouth are used to promote these auditions.

If you want to try your hand at acting, join a theater class or group. The first step is generally an audition, where you present a brief prepared speech or scripted scene from the play for the director. For some parts, performers with a powerful singing voice are needed, and you may need to practice a quick song acapella or supply your own background music. There is usually a packet of information or description of requirements in the advertisement for public auditions.

A lot of amateur theater companies hold open casting calls. While participating in community theater can help players build their skills and knowledge, most pro theaters prefer to cast performers who have completed an approved training course. You can register at a university theatrical department or take private acting lessons from seasoned theater performers. While some theater majors may pursue a Master of Fine Arts degree before joining the competitive acting field, others may pursue a professional job after graduating with a Bachelor of Arts degree. Some may opt for the chance to study theater history and theatrical training to familiarize themselves with the physical and mental requirements of the profession.

It may be difficult to break into the world of professional theatrical acting, so many aspiring actors find alternative ways to make a living. Actors' schedules must also allow for flexibility because their roles in professional theatre productions may require travel or a busy performance schedule.

Some performers find it simpler to launch their careers in the local theater scene. A lot of professional theater companies only recruit union actors, and many performers are encouraged to join the local actor's association or union. A budding actor can also look for a capable manager or talent agency who can arrange auditions and connect actors with knowledgeable producers and directors. Theater acting requires close collaboration between many participants to produce a successful show. Anyone interested in acting should be ready to work on the side because it's often a world of feast or famine.

VOLUNTEER TO READ ALOUD IN CLASS

If you want to get better at public speaking and enjoy it more, you have an option sitting before you every day you're in a classroom. You can volunteer to read aloud at the teacher's request.

If you've ever been in a class that requires reading, you undoubtedly remember the teacher calling on students to read out loud. Whether you're reading a history book or The Lord of the Rings, class is a perfect place for budding performers to practice reading out loud.

While reading aloud, you'll bring your full attention to the current task without distractions. You're likely to be so concentrated that you won't even be aware that your linguistic abilities are improving.

Your mind is like a muscle. Whenever you read in class, you exercise the link between your mind and voice, leading to better coherence and performance.

When you read a lengthy chapter or a paragraph in class or any other setting in front of others, strong focus and cohesion is necessary for good performance. Reading aloud to others gives you more respect and understanding of the written word and what it means, including intent and purpose. In other words, you gain a better understand of each word's function and context by reading aloud. You'll find yourself putting more effort into writing strong, purposeful content for your speeches.

When anything is read aloud, it sounds more intentional and significant. Words are refined and have increased potency when they're projected with the human voice. Reading aloud brings the words into focus as well as the speaker's tone and inflection.

Have you ever seen a written term you weren't sure how to pronounce when there's no dictionary in sight? Reading aloud increases your vocabulary. Speaking something in context helps you discern meaning.

When you read silently, you only hear the phrases internally, and their impact is only as great as your interpretation of the text. The words may have more significance when read aloud because you assess possible meanings, deciding the ones that fit best. This is part of how new words enter your vocabulary, improving your use of language.

You acquire the thrill of learning the melodies of words you haven't used before, in addition to expanding your spoken repertoire. After all, words are more than just their definitions. Words are frequently combined because they sound nice when arranged in a particular way. A new term is a discovery—as if you've found a priceless gem. There are new words just waiting to be discovered and added to your vocabulary, but you have to look for them.

Some folks amass recipes, old automobiles, or hockey cards, and some people amass words.

Reading books from different eras, topics you don't know much about, or from far-off locales offers you a style tour while increasing your vocabulary. A dictionary should always be handy if you wish to expand your vocabulary. This will help you a lot when you're creating your speech and perfecting it. You want to use strong, powerful words that ring out to get your point across. You don't want to see the same words again and again and again.

Read a lot, expand your vocabulary, and challenge yourself to learn new words and phrases. Doing this will not only make you smarter—it will make you a better public speaker too.

Reading aloud in class can improve your performing abilities, which helps you become a better public speaker. When reading aloud, avoid monotony, especially if there's an audience. Make use of your entire vocal range. You can better understand and explore your range by expressing words as though you really want them to be heard.

If you're unsure of how you come across while speaking, record and listen to the audio to hear where your voice rises and falls, begins and stops, varies or catches you off guard. Speech patterns are important because they structure language usage and how it is perceived.

To control your tone and vocal strength, mark the written word with a highlighter. You'll be astounded at the difference a little planning and attention can make in your presentation. Think of yourself as your own director, and experiment with variety in your delivery.

Color your words with emotion, meaning, and understanding when your intonation is regulated. The easiest way to give text your personal flair is through inflection, which is sounding distinctive and enthusiastic.

Think of the best performances you've heard. Examine what it was that really spoke to you. What did you love about them? Take notes, and apply them to your own reading style.

By doing all this and reading aloud, you will get better at understanding the written word and how you relay it. This will make you much better at public speaking. It will turn you into a performer in class and also make you more of a director, author, critic, and all-around great performer.

Get comfortable reading aloud in front of others because it will turn public speaking into a rewarding joy.

CHAPTER FIVE:

DEBATE CLUB

Are you familiar with the debate club at school? Maybe. Maybe not. The truth is that debate clubs aren't as prevalent and popular as they once were, yet there are many high schools that still have them.

Many people don't understand debate club, and honestly, it's not for everyone. It requires a lot of work, knowledge, research, and more. Some people think it's not worth their time.

That's fine and good for them, but for many other people, debate club is something that helps them get better at public speaking. It will help them feel more comfortable talking in front of strangers or classmates. It will help them study better, write better, criticize, and analyze better. In many ways, debate club is the best way to figure out how to talk in public and get your point across. In fact, debate clubs are built around this idea. It even rewards you for making a better point than your opponent.

Think about it: Giving a public speech is about getting your point across and winning people over to your side by convincing them of your statements. Debate club is a great place to hone those skills to become more confident speaking to others. Debate club isn't just about being persuasive; it's about convincing others and making them see your point. This is done by understanding how to communicate clearly and decisively.

Debate club is a great place for any teen trying to be better at public speaking. It's a wonderful place to learn about research, tone, writing engaging content, and winning people over. Many people turn to debate club to become better public speakers with enhanced understanding, develop control of language, and learn how to convince a crowd.

HOW TO
PRACTICE DEBATE

Debating is a very good skill to have in your pocket. Good argumentative skills lead to a variety of advantages, including career success, leadership opportunities, and academic accomplishment. More than that, it helps you speak in public. You will learn to master facts with confidence, control, tone, and calmness. If you're unsure of how to debate effectively, there are many things to remember when perfecting your skills and technique.

In a debate, you compete to win by setting forth the strongest possible case. Although they can take place in casual contexts, debates are typically formal.

In a debate, a remark is made, and members then select a positive or negative stance. Participants in a debate have time to get ready before arguing their case for a specified amount of time. A judge decides which side made the strongest points after speakers from each side alternate turns.

Consider assigning each speaker responsibility for one aspect of the debate, such as sociological, legal, or economic factors. If you're presenting numerous reasons, start your speech with the most convincing one, no matter what format you choose.

A crucial step in the argument process is the rebuttal. A team's claim is disproven if it can dissect the other team's supporting documentation.

How do you prepare for a debate? You prepare in many of the same ways you would for a speech in front of an audience. Keep in mind that being on a team involves cooperating with one another. Make sure your ideas flow together and adhere to a logical progression by reading one another's speeches, practicing in front of each other, and reading and delivering each other's speeches.

Have each team member come up with their own ideas before you get together. This enables your team to gather a wider range of arguments and choose the most important ones to feature in your presentation.

By demonstrating that you possess the best supporting evidence, you will prevail in the discussion. Make sure your proof is correct and demonstrable by checking it three times. Collect a variety of sources to support your claims.

Speech preparation is crucial to your success. Have your colleagues review your writing and schedule regular team discussions so that everyone is aware of potential argument outcomes.

Recognize that every second you spend putting your strategy together gets you one step ahead of the competition. You'll appear confident by referencing your data and maintaining eye contact.

THE BENEFITS
OF DEBATING

Striving to be a skilled debater has several advantages, including learning how to research, use logic, and speak in public. Debating can help you face any problem by teaching you how to plan your case, even if you disagree with it, and carefully choose your words.

Despite what some people say, debating is not the same as getting into an argument. Quite the opposite, in fact. Instead of assaulting your opponent without thinking, you're building a strong, succinct case that will win backing and approval.

While you might not have a dispute every day, you almost certainly will have disagreements in life. You may be able to avoid an argument by debating rather than arguing. If needed, take a few steps back and consider your comments before speaking up.

Through debate, you improve your critical thinking abilities, which are necessary in everyday life as well as in public speaking. Critical thinking is the capacity to formulate well-reasoned arguments while simultaneously challenging the veracity of supporting data.

Debate will help you develop a healthy attitude by creating an interest in new ideas while simultaneously encouraging you to remain skeptical. You'll learn to be modest since you won't always be correct.

Debating assists in determining your target audience and the best tone to use while discussing any topic. A formal tone could alienate your audience, while a casual tone might call into question any arguments you attempt to make.

Every debater needs the ability to prepare and express their ideas clearly to construct a persuasive case, even if you don't agree with the points made because of your principles. Another key element is the delivery of your speech. Every successful debate should include establishing eye contact and maintaining your composure.

The way you put your argument together is equally important. Your justifications should be logical and well organized. The fundamental skills you have developed through education—finding and reading sources, planning and composing speeches, and speaking with confidence—are things that skilled debaters depend on.

Think beyond your usual horizons, question your adversaries, and look for weaknesses in their counterarguments. Thinking twice might cost you valuable time and points during a debate, so reacting quickly to remarks and questions is important.

Learn to accept defeat with grace and take responsibility for your weaknesses. Long term, this will help you become a more skilled and polished speaker.

In every discussion, effective speakers demonstrate empathy. Compassion enables you to understand the opinions of those who agree with your argument, even if you disagree with the one you were assigned. While you are not required to accept the opposing viewpoint, having empathy for others will benefit your interpersonal interactions.

Skilled debaters maintain calm and poise, focusing on the topic before them instead of allowing it to distract them. The ability to control your emotions is a skill that will benefit you in many areas of life beyond debate.

By honing your debate techniques, you'll also be able to make sense of complex issues. If you thoroughly investigate the subject and create the arguments you want to make, you'll be able to construct a superior case on most any subject. Finding answers to issues and compiling innovative solutions is crucial for any successful debater.

People gain fresh perspectives on the world via debate. Students learn about subjects in debate they otherwise might not consider, giving them a broader grasp of culture and the world we live in. A broader perspective may inspire you to value your current prospects and past successes.

Debate helps your skills and outlook on life, the world, and other people. It's a great way to learn about caring, compassion, and thoughtfulness. Debate teaches you about the world around you and the people you interact with. One of the biggest benefits of debate club is becoming a speaker who is calm, collected, clear headed, well spoken, and able to deftly express an argument.

HIRING
A DEBATE COACH

In the realm of debate, private coaching has become popular. If you pay attention to the world of debate, you've seen a rise in the number of private coaches available to students in need of extra support and enhanced debate skills.

Students seek individual coaching for a variety of reasons, including strategy formulation, skill practice, pre-debate coaching, and judging requirements. Independent debaters make up a large portion of students who desire private coaching, but there are students who seek out mentoring just to advance their skills. Coaches have the expertise, knowledge, and skills to help you become a better debater.

Over the last few years, many people who want to become better public speakers have hired debate coaches to perfect their skills. The biggest reason is that debate coaches are generally less expensive than other public speaking experts, and they're usually more willing to work one on one to teach you how to be a better speaker.

PRACTICE DEBATING BOTH SIDES OF AN ARGUMENT

One of the most important skills to learn about debate is remembering that there are two sides to every argument. This will make you a better debater, speaker, and communicator. In fact, you should educate yourself on both sides of every debate you participate in, which means you'll have a better viewpoint of the entire situation, not just the side you're defending.

If you believe in what you say and want to convince others to do the same, study both sides of every debate, which will give you more information and test your beliefs about the argument at hand. This solidifies your opinions and leads to better performances. When you believe in what you're saying, it will come through with passion, energy, and enthusiasm.

DEBATING
ON STAGE

Imagine that you've studied how to debate and taken the expertise of a coach to heart. You've read all about debating and focused on what you need to remember when facing off against your opponent. Remember that being good at debating will also make you good at public speaking.

So, you're ready for the big debate, but you should once again review your checklist to remember everything when you're on stage. Being on stage for your debate can bring up issues that made you afraid of public speaking in the first place. You will see your opponent, the crowd, and the moderators and judges. All eyes will be watching, and you'll have attention you might be uncomfortable with.

All that noise in your head can get in the way, so it's vital to remember a few important things when you're about to open your mouth. Follow the debate steps you've been trained in, go get 'em, and win the day.

You need thorough comprehension of your subject and the ability to think quickly if you want to come across as an expert and communicate intelligently. In a debate, the moderator or the other side may ask questions, and a skeptical audience may put you through a challenging question-and-answer session. You'll be ready for everything that comes at you if you know your stuff. But understanding your arguments is only half the battle. You should be able to refute the opponent's points, which requires you to understand the other side's stance. The crowd's beliefs may vary from your own, and you have to refute their viewpoints *and* persuade them of the validity and strength of your arguments.

Everyone's attention will be on you during the debate, so maintain your poise and stand up straight. Be mindful of your body language in response to your opponent's assertions. Eye rolling or pursed lips will be interpreted as disrespectful or hostile. Remember that you're being observed even if you aren't actively debating.

Your debate allows the audience to hear your ideas and understand your points. It's easy to get swept up in the feelings of the moment in a stressful situation. However, agitation won't help your cause, so maintain your composure even if your adversary or the audience tries to provoke you. Being calm and collected will help you gain the respect of others.

Avoid attempting to replicate the absence of visual assistance like the presidential debates, which is one of the factors that sets them apart from most presentations. Visual aids support the spoken word and help you make your points. They are remembered more readily and processed more quickly than spoken words.

Always remember that the purpose of any debate is to persuade and convince the audience that you have the best points and know what you're talking about. When your message is clear, the audience is much more likely to understand and hold your perspective. Maintain control to successfully demonstrate your authority and competence on your topic.

You need to be aware of how you look and come off to the audience. The performance aspect of debate is an important part of your success. It's the difference between winning and losing for many debaters.

As you can see, debate is a great way to excel at public speaking. If you can master debating, you can master speaking. If you're comfortable debating on a stage, why wouldn't you be comfortable giving a speech in front of a group of fellow students?

CHAPTER SIX:

SPEAKING ON TOPICS

Your teacher will most likely dictate the topic you'll be speaking about. Increasingly, however, teachers are allowing students to figure out their own speech topics.

So, let's say you're assigned to speak on a topic of your own choice. What will it be, and how do you decide? How do you find an appropriate topic that gives you enough material to dig into? Let's dive right in because there's a lot to think about when searching for the right topic for a speech.

CHOOSING A TOPIC TO SPEAK ABOUT

Choosing a speech topic is a tall order for new public speakers. To make it easier, your teacher might give you a few guidelines. You may be asked to tell a story about a moment that changed your life or give an example of how to do something specific. In this section, we'll discuss typical public speaking limitations, choosing a topic area, and whittling it down to a size that fits your time limit.

Every speaker is constrained by certain rules. For instance, student speakers are frequently assigned to address a specific subject. This means you're not free to choose another subject, so whatever you do, always stay on topic.

When planning your presentation, you'll have a fixed amount of time to make your points. You may even have your time cut short at the last minute, so be prepared for any eventuality. The four main limitations that can occur are purpose, audience, context, and time.

The overall objective of the speech is the first limitation that you may experience. The three general objectives of any speech are to inform, convince, and entertain. You will be precluded from giving a presentation designed to influence or entertain the audience if you've been assigned an educational presentation. In most cases, teachers will outline the precise goal of every presentation you give.

The group you speak to is the second limitation. Your chances of giving a successful speech increase the more you know the audience. Naturally, the best method to select an appropriate topic is to know as much as possible about the audience. If you can't learn much, at least make sure you don't say anything that may offend the group. As a guideline, think of what might ruffle feathers or upset people in your class. If you're required to speak about a topic that could upset people, make sure you do it gently, and be as respectful as possible.

Context is another significant limitation. The ideas around a situation (i.e., your speech) are its context. You may find yourself speaking in a variety of settings, and expectations for the speaker are likely to vary in each. In a business class, a subject suitable for an English class might not work. If your assignment is giving your life story, talking about the history of South America won't be appropriate. Remember what class you're speaking in and what the specific assignment is.

The length of your speech will be the final limitation you encounter. For presentations that are under ten minutes, carefully limit your topic to one main concept. For instance, it would be unrealistic to think you can cover the Battle of Gettysburg in a ten-minute lecture. It's not possible to condense all that material into ten minutes when there are innumerable tomes and dissertations that cover the subject.

Instead, focus on a topic that can be realistically handled in the allotted time. If you are tasked with writing about the Battle of Gettysburg, the most you can do in ten minutes is give a brief overview explaining why the battle was significant to the American Civil War of the 1860s.

If you pick your own topic, you have a wide list of topics to choose from. Once you know your limitations, you can start considering topics. The first thing to think about is the area you're interested in. A topic could be a vast field of study. Examples of subjects include the humanities, science, history, art, and education. Cast a wide net when choosing a topic, which will help you narrow down and eliminate options.

Additionally, there are many subtopics that fall under each larger subject category. The topic of art can be divided into broad groups like primitive art, Renaissance art, Impressionism, and modern art. These broad categories can be further divided into more specific subject areas.

It takes effort and experience to narrow your subject to something workable for your time restrictions. A major mistake novice presenters make is not focusing on a limited enough subject given the time limit assigned.

Narrowing your subject is like a funnel. Large subject categories are at the top of the funnel, and your objective is to limit your topic until you have just enough to flow smoothly through the narrow end of the funnel. Your speech will be simpler to research, prepare, and present when your topic fits your time limit.

WRITING YOUR SPEECH

Okay, the time has come. It is time to write your speech. Writing is the most important part of any public speaking assignment. Obviously, you want to do a great job speaking, but you can't do that if you don't do a good writing job to begin with.

Writing isn't easy for everyone. Sometimes, it's not even easy for talented writers. It takes knowledge, planning, and creativity. Keep in mind that less is more if you want to keep the attention of your listeners. Shorter is preferable than longer. It's better to thoroughly cover a few key ideas than to cover a lot of topics superficially.

Another excellent piece of advice is that it's difficult to memorize a whole speech word for word. Instead, make a presentation plan and employ literary techniques to beef up your material. Examples and stories are excellent ways to support your arguments. Start by limiting your topic. Use the five Ws from journalism: who, what, when, where, and why. This is a simple approach that covers most of your preparation.

If you're having trouble focusing your topic, start with the last W, the *why*. Why should your fellow students be interested in the subject you're discussing? Why should they listen to you and not just turn to their phones or the nearby open window? Your speech will be better focused and engaging if you answer the Ws in your speech.

Create a detailed speech outline of your key points once you select a suitable topic. When writing the body of your speech, make a list of the concepts and details that best describe the subject. Once you create a list of crucial elements, order them by importance, starting with the most significant. Then rank them in order of importance.

You won't be able to address every idea you brainstorm. Only three or four of the most important items should be covered. One topic or bullet should be covered for every five minutes of your time allotment. Restrict yourself to no more than five topics. Three points is a suitable quantity for a brief speech, which is probably what you'll cover for most class projects.

There's a difference between what you want to cover and what you have time to cover. Many people erroneously put secondary bullet points in their outlines. In fact, they may fill it up with dozens of them. For whatever reason, many students believe that using a lot of additional bullet points means that the noted information is essential to everyone.

This is also a mistake that makes many speeches tedious and challenging to perform. It causes your speech to lose focus. You may think that many little scintillating points drive your point home, but the opposite is true. They make your speech seem rambling and unfocused. That's a one-way ticket to losing your audience and getting a bad grade.

Don't forget to portray yourself well. You're not just a speaker when you give a speech; you're also an entertainer. At the outset, describe yourself or give an example from your life that tells the audience who you are.

Don't let the personal stories stop there. Try to think of personal anecdotes you can relay that are linked to the topic at hand. Tell a brief account of something that happened to you, family members, or friends. These examples provide compelling evidence that what you say is accurate. It's ironic that many presenters steer clear of personal stories. Professional presenters, however, often rely on anecdotal events to illustrate their points and keep the audience's attention.

Sometimes, a quote from a well-known public figure can add credibility to your speech. You can use a quote to emphasize points you want your audience to remember.

There are other literary tricks of the trade to use in your speech. For example, an analogy may spice up your speech and help you remember your arguments by using a real-life example to demonstrate your major themes and ideas. Analogies help to contrast a point you want to make using examples that underscore your points.

HOW TO OPEN
A SPEECH

The success of your presentation depends largely on the opening sequence. Your opening remarks should be as captivating as possible. If you capture your audience right at the beginning, chances are you'll have them for the duration of your speech. If you don't grab their attention early, it will be harder to get later. Start with a bang to keep people engaged as long as you keep the momentum going.

Give them a reason to believe their time commitment will be worthwhile. Pull them in, keep them invested, and make sure they're engaged by starting with a great opener.

Do you recall a time when someone you didn't know showed compassion or good advice had a tremendous impact on you? Suggest to your audience they could be just a few seconds away from discovering something substantial and powerful. The thought of learning a priceless nugget is an ideal lead-in to capture and hold audience attention. Go deep, and be vulnerable with real emotional honesty. It's more than okay to be open. The audience will want to learn why that moment had such a strong impact on you.

The human condition is communicated effectively via stories. Relay a tale you've known for years, or choose one from the newspaper or a favorite website. Avoid starting your tale with, "Boy, do I have a story for you." Simply begin with the story. This is better because it will draw people in, predisposing them to listen empathically.

You can also ask a question that defies logic, yields an unexpected result, or adds a surprising element. The audience can be persuaded to reevaluate previously held opinions or ideas by using the same tactic. To move seamlessly from audience responses to the point you're attempting to make, you need to be fast on your feet and quick minded.

Why not start your speech with a mystery? Detective stories and psychological thrillers that readers and viewers can't get enough of are always popular, so using this approach for your speech can make it even better. A mystery is also suitable for your opening as well. Here's one approach: Commence your speech with just one question, and at some point, answer it in pieces, saving the major revelation for the end.

Multiple-choice questions are always popular in school exams, and a multiple-choice opening in your speech can also be popular as well. Start your speech by presenting a question with several possible answers, such as, "What would you do if you met a stranger who offered you a million dollars? Would you: a) accept it without question, b) ask where the money came from or, c) run in the other direction?" You can pose any number of questions or scenarios to your audience. This opening is ideal for a discussion with several points of view on a subject or various approaches to the same subject. It's also a wonderful way to draw people in and make them think deep thoughts or question themselves and their worldview.

Distortions, brain teasers, tricks, and other riddles have a way of grabbing attention across most age spectrums. If you start your speech with an opener that gets people questioning things, you'll have their attention for a while. Be careful with this type of opening, though, because it could get people too fired up and hard to settle down. After that, paying attention to the rest of your speech could go out the window.

Do you recall a speaker whose joke ended up becoming one of your favorites? You can't go wrong making your audience laugh when you start a speech. To start in this manner, you need to know how to handle comedy. Folks who poke fun and also laugh at themselves tend to be nice and humble, which are both qualities that appeal to audiences. If you're going to laugh at yourself, be sure it won't cost you anything. Avoid making jokes that undermine your authority or the subject of your speech. Also, watch out for showing self-pity with self-deprecating humor. People want to laugh with you, not at you.

FIND AN EVENT TO SPEAK ABOUT YOUR FAVORITE TOPICS

Finding places for teens to talk about the things they love is harder than you'd expect. You'd think there would be plenty of venues where teens could give a talk. Everyone loves encouraging teenagers to speak on various subjects, especially the most popular subjects of the day. However, it's not always as easy as you think.

But there are ways for students to go out in the world to practice their public speaking skills. There are quite a few ways for teens to try out the public speaking skills that are changing their lives, making them more confident and social.

If you attend a local church or religious organization, chances are they would be more than willing to get the perspective of a teenager. You'd also have a supportive audience at those locations. An audience at a religious organization won't be a tough crowd; they'll make you feel welcome and accepted, which can give you a lot more confidence.

How often do you go to the local library? You should go more often, but perhaps the most important reason to go to the library is they regularly hold events and classes there. And guess what? They are all free of charge.

The library will give you plenty of chances to speak. If you're attending a class there, at some point you will ask a question. It doesn't matter what it is, but you *will* ask something. Yes, this puts a little bit of pressure on you, but it will also make you feel more comfortable speaking in front of others.

Nearly every town in the country has a city council. Its city leaders come together, discuss important topics, and vote on the most pressing issues at hand. It's a great place for a young, driven teen to speak their mind to a rapt audience.

The thing about all city council meetings is that leaders are eager for the public to attend and give their opinions. You can come in and speak about a number of things related to upcoming laws, events, and issues affecting the community. Speaking at a city council meeting is a great way for a teen to practice public speaking. Why? Because your audience will be respectful and pay attention. You'll have to stay on topic there. In fact, if you go off topic, you're liable to have your mic cut. You'll also have a time limit, so preparation is important.

Another great reason for budding speakers to talk at city council is they can effect change and help the community around them. So, why wouldn't you want to practice your speaking skills by doing something good for the city and its citizens?

Look up your next city council meeting's agenda to see if there's an item there you'd like to comment on. Is there an issue there that fires you up? If so, write up a short speech and go change the world!

There is yet another option for young student speakers looking to get better at their public speaking skills. But be warned that it sometimes strikes fear into the hearts of students: a job fair.

Job fairs are a great place to search if you want to be hired by a company that wants you to do public speaking. There are quite a few jobs that require public speaking, although you might not expect it.

Call centers are a great place to work where you literally talk for a living. Plus, you'll have to speak with strangers, stay on topic, and not ramble too much—all important things to learn when speaking in public.

There are other jobs that require you to speak in public with authority, knowledge, and personality. Those jobs require knowledge about communication and other specific topics related to your field of work. Unsurprisingly, these jobs will also enhance your social skills and your ease speaking to strangers. When you go to a job fair, think of each possible employer as an opportunity to improve your skills talking to others about a variety of topics. When you look at it that way, you'll see that public speaking opportunities are everywhere.

Of course, social media has made finding audiences easier than ever. So, if you're a teenager with a need and the desire to perfect your public speaking skills, hop on the site you're probably already on multiple times a day: Facebook. Once there, look for local youth groups, causes, and more. You can find a number of events and groups that are looking for speakers or participants. Each of them is a chance to get better at talking with people and enhancing your social skills too.

CREATE SHOWS
FOR TEEN SPEAKERS
AT COMMUNITY CENTERS

Say there aren't a lot of places in your city for teens to speak. You've already tried your hand at religious centers, job fairs, city council meetings, and more. Yet you are still left wanting more. Not only that, maybe the idea of public speaking has become more than just a hobby. It's now something that really appeals to you, something you can see yourself pursuing as a career in the future.

If that's the case, you may want to create an event that will call upon other speakers to come together and bring in a crowd to let everyone enjoy the power of public speaking. A side benefit is that it could create a lot of contacts for you in the industry even at a young age.

There are things to keep in mind if you're throwing a speaking event. For starters, you'll need to find a venue. Being a teenager will work to your advantage here because many event locations and businesses will support a student throwing such an event, so they may cut you some slack when it comes to budget, pricing, and more.

Once you find your location, treat the planning aspect like a full-time job. You'll need to buckle down and focus on making the event the best of the best.

Create a hashtag that your staff and guests use to advertise your event on social media before, during, and after it happens. Your hashtag should be original, succinct, and pertinent. Check to see whether the hashtag you want is used by other events or companies. Then show off and promote it on the website for your speaking event, plus any social media pages related to you or the event. What's more, add it to newsletters, emails, local media, and other channels before your event series. Remember that we live in the age of social media, and unless you have a hashtag for your event, no one will pay attention to it or talk about it.

Urge the event speakers who have agreed to attend to interact with participants on the web, and encourage attendees to submit pictures of it on various social media platforms. To further promote online involvement, consider including an account on Twitter, Instagram, TikTok, and more. If your event is on Facebook, make sure you create a group page for it so that people can talk about the event with one another. Allowing participants to interact online creates a sense of continuity between events that will keep people loyal and drawn to the event as if it's their own.

You can also build a community utilizing a networking site such as LinkedIn. By understanding more about the event, attendees can network with one another. You may also have a Google recap or publish a newsletter informing readers about the speakers, seminars, and exhibitors that will be at each event.

Make sure the entire event, including registration, goes as smoothly as possible. The use of event-registration software allows organizers to connect with participants to find out more about their preferences. For the management of your event series, you will need information from registrants. When people sign up for the event, they will submit personal information that you can access. You may infer a person's preferences from details like age, gender, and home address. You can better meet the demands of your attendees by making modifications with the use of this information.

There are several trustworthy organizations that offer knowledgeable speakers in various industries. However, those in charge of planning events on a limited budget should think about asking local business professors to speak.

Of course, since you're a student throwing the speaking event, you'll want other students involved too. You'll probably find a few at your own school if you reach out, talk to them, and offer them a prime spot in your speaking event. Make sure they get involved and engaged. It is important that young speakers tell their families and friends and post about it on social media. They won't be paid, but perhaps you can talk to your high school about possibly getting extra credit.

Reach out to local businesses for sponsorship of your event, which is a great way to make money to pay for your expenses. Tell them the purpose of the event, who is involved, and why you're doing it. It will be hard for businesses to turn you away when they see your enthusiasm and the premise behind your event. You're likely to receive donations in the form of money or products. Getting support will involve talk to new people, and you can practice your public speaking skills yet again.

Keep the cost of the event in mind because events become very expensive very fast, which is the last thing you want to deal with as a student. Since hosting a series of events will be pricier than planning a single event, think about choosing locations close to universities to reduce speaking fees and make it simpler to provide guests with information and accommodations.

Find a theme to tie the event together. Make sure that all speakers will touch upon certain subject matters, and come up with a flow for the entire day. Set up a schedule that allows each speech to lend itself to the next. For example, a speaker might mention the next speech at the conclusion of theirs, outlining issues that will be covered, the names of participating speakers, and so on.

It's simpler to persuade current attendees to attend future events by organizing an event series around distinct topics, and it will also be simpler for event planners to arrange.

Lastly, you need to be a bit selfish when you are putting together your speaking event. This means that you should look out for yourself, your future, and your public speaking skills. Give yourself a good spot in the schedule and a great topic to talk about. Do whatever you need to make this an event that will work best for you and your public speaking persona. Remember that this is about you. You put it together, you did the hard work, and you are the reason the whole thing is happening. It may be a public speaking event for many others, but it should always be *your* event too.

CHAPTER SEVEN:

SPEAKING
IN SCHOOL

Speaking in school can be a nerve-racking, intense experience. For some people, it's too much. For others, it's very rewarding. No matter how a student feels about speaking in school, they know that it's a big deal. It's been done by students for generations, and it won't stop with you. So, if you are afraid of speaking in public, you need to work on overcoming it.

The following pointers will help you more than you think, and you'll find that speaking in class isn't nearly as scary you're imagining it to be.

PRACTICE READING
YOUR SPEECH ALOUD

Your narrow vocabulary causes you to repeatedly employ a small set of terms in your regular life. However, you cover a considerably wider vocabulary when you read aloud from a book or newspaper. This happens because reading aloud enhances fluency, and you use a greater range of spoken sounds.

Because the English language happens to be non-phonetic, words aren't necessarily pronounced the same way they're written. This means that perfecting English pronunciation requires work, and one of the most effective activities for speech improvement is reading aloud.

Reading aloud regularly serves as a review for pronunciation techniques and the speaking skills you're acquiring. Speaking words aloud is an excellent exercise to help train your brain to pronounce new words. When you come across a new word for the first time, repeat the pronunciation as you read the text aloud.

READ AS
YOU WRITE

If you really want to create a piece of public speaking that will feel natural, you need to think ahead about your delivery and how you want it to sound. If you read aloud as you write, it'll all flow easily and naturally when you are finally delivering your speech.

We've all seen that scene in a movie where someone is typing something and reading aloud as they go. They say every word as they hit the keys. Honestly, a movie situation like that might look kind of hokey, but when you do it in real life, you'll find it helps.

When you read aloud as you write, you're much more likely to write in your own voice. When you're reading your work to yourself as you create it, everything will feel more authentic and more like you. A public speech needs to come from the heart and feel personal the way you created it.

USE YOUR NORMAL SPEAKING VOICE

Some people make the mistake of feeling like they're on a Broadway stage when they speak publicly. They puff up their chests, project like they're speaking to thousands of people, and put on a persona that feels pretentious.

When you deliver your speech, remember that you are *you*. You're not someone hired by your teacher to talk about the subject.

The only voice and persona you need to present during a speech is your own. Don't change your voice or your personality. Instead, just raise your voice a bit and speak clearly with confidence and authority about your subject.

Your posture is important when you speak in class because it helps you project in a natural way. When you stand straight, you breathe more easily and you'll speak from your diaphragm.

If you are naturally a soft-spoken person, there are ways to project your voice so that your audience can hear you. Most people don't know that your voice is powered by your breath. Your voice will be louder and stronger the more oxygen you take in. Learning how to breathe deeply and properly is important to understanding good breath control. There is no doubt that your breathing habits have an impact on how you sound. You have a voice because air passes across your vocal cords, after all.

Weak breathing causes you to run out of air, which causes your throat muscles to contract in an effort to force out sound. Any voice will be strained and weak without proper (deep) breathing. It's also difficult on the vocal cords and can cause serious damage to them over time.

You'll have to breathe deeper with additional breaths if you want to loudly project your voice. Whenever you inhale fully, your voice is supported by an air cushion, allowing your throat muscles to remain at ease. This will make your voice sound fuller, more engaging, and more pleasant to the ear. It will be more appealing and carry better too.

Most people breathe into the top of their lungs; however, your lungs expand more at the base. Look at yourself in a mirror and breathe deeply. Did you lift your shoulders? Did you notice any strain in your jaw or neck? If so, read on to discover effective breathing techniques.

You should completely fill your lungs as you take a deep inhale. The waist and belly have to expand as you inhale and retract when you exhale. Your chest shouldn't move as your lungs expand. Musicians who play wind instruments understand this concept very well.

Picture yourself filling your lungs with water rather than air. Put your hands on your stomach. As you breathe properly, your stomach should push out, and you should be able to feel it. As you talk, hold your hands in that same spot so that you can sense the air escape. Now, place your hands flat on your back, right below the level of your ribs. Take a big breath in, and visualize your hands lifting as you continue to inhale.

After you've taken the breath, practice producing the sound. Try making a sound with your large, full breath. Say *AH* or *EE* while picturing the sound emanating from your back behind your rib cage. Do this several times. Put some serious air behind the sound.

You may not be aware that how clearly you speak affects how loudly you speak. Your jaw, lips, and tongue are the instruments you need to speak clearly. To produce loud, distinct sounds, you exert a lot of effort when using those instruments.

Your voice will rise away from your neck muscles and into your face as you exert energy into your articulation muscles. In reality, your voice enters the sinuses and cheekbones. Your nasal cavities reverberate like a large, empty chamber, and your cheekbones operate like a piano's sounding board. As a result, your voice will travel stronger to your audience with greater resonance.

Consider how much energy is required to run the entire length of a basketball court or soccer field. It takes the same amount of work to articulate clearly, but you utilize fewer muscles.

When you think about it, projecting isn't that hard, but it is that vital. With a little bit of practice, and paying attention to how your body looks and feels when you speak from deep inside, you will soon be able to project out to a wide, engaged audience.

ADOPT CONFIDENT BODY LANGUAGE

Confidence is very important for many reasons when you give a public speech. The audience needs to believe that the person speaking really believes what they're saying. When *you* believe in the statements you make, others will as well. Confidence is the key to making people believe you know what you're talking about.

Confidence also helps you feel better when you speak to an audience. When you appear confident, your entire attitude will ease, and you will be relaxed and comfortable as you present.

Did you know that body language is a big part of being, feeling, and looking confident? It's true. When you hold your body in certain ways, your speaking experience becomes easier. Even if you're not naturally a confident person, you soon will be because you hold yourself differently and do things in a new way.

Maintain eye contact throughout your speech to convey confidence. Move your eyes from one audience member to another, and connect with as many as possible. Maintaining eye contact conveys attention and comfort to those around you. If making eye contact with someone is too daunting, start by focusing on a region around their eyes. Usually, people can't tell the difference from a distance.

Remember not to seem casual with your body language. People who struggle with social anxiety frequently try to occupy the least amount of space, which typically results in slumping defensively. You don't want to come across that way when you're on stage. Uncross your arms and legs, move your shoulders back from your ears, and make sure to

posture

straighten your back. Taking up space makes you appear self-assured.

Keep your head high, and walk with your gaze front and center, looking confident. Although it may seem awkward at first, you will get used to this very assured posture. Later, you may even choose to speak like this all the time, even when you aren't giving a speech.

A clear indication of anxiousness and uneasiness is fidgeting. Reduce fidgeting to appear more assured. Nervous gestures like drumming your fingers on the table or bouncing your knee detract from your speech and make it difficult for listeners to concentrate on your message.

Even though it may be tempting to put your hands in your pockets, especially if you are concerned that they might shake, it makes you appear more tense and uneasy, even if it's something you do all of the time. If you want to appear more confident, keep your hands out of your pockets during your speech.

Avoid placing your hands on your face or neck as you speak, since both these things show fear, apprehension, or nervousness. However, holding your palms out almost always conveys confidence to those watching you.

We usually behave unconsciously in certain ways, such as sitting up taller when friends are present or using our hands more often when among others who do the same. Mirroring someone else's body language demonstrates your interest in them, which may increase comprehension and help develop a bond. You feel more at ease and self-assured when you sense that connection.

Still unsure whether you can gain the confidence necessary to alter your body language? Keep in mind that you don't need to be self-assured to alter your body language. Acting with confidence may seem unusual at first, but it will ultimately seem more natural and improve your self-esteem.

CHAPTER EIGHT:

THEATRE

Before any sort of performance from acting on stage to giving a speech to just speaking in front of family or friends, actors and public speakers need to learn how to control their tension and anxiety. Many are shocked to learn that using your diaphragm as a stress reliever is quite helpful. For many individuals, anxiety and presenting in front of groups always appear together.

The fact is that overcoming your fear, or stifling it, is not necessary to become a courageous, accomplished, lifelong public speaker. It involves converting dread into vigor and enthusiasm. Basic breathing exercises or relaxation techniques can significantly reduce your anxiety.

Those in the know understand that terrific, talented speakers and actors don't pretend. Both must be genuine and present their genuine selves to the audience. Authenticity equates to charisma and magnetism, or what critics and theatregoers often refer to as "presence." Learn to feel at ease in the limelight before giving a presentation. This entails acknowledging your key function as a speaker. You can sense that some speakers feel uneasy with that degree of scrutiny, and you can't really blame them; it's a bit intense to have so many people paying such close attention to you. That's why so many suffer from stage fright.

Public speaking, however, is a show much like being on the stage, and if you can handle theatre, you can handle public speaking. You won't be able to spread your words and ideas to your teacher and your class if you don't get comfortable speaking to a live audience.

In every type of performance, you need to know how you hold your body and carry yourself. And yes, a key component of good public speaking is body language. However, understanding body language doesn't involve memorizing a set of guidelines for when and where to position your arms and feet.

Powerful body language originates within you and begins with your own mindset. It should come as no shock that fellow students paying attention to you will be greatly impacted by the way you present yourself.

Become adept at using space. In theatre, space is naturally the stage and set around you. When it comes to giving a speech, space might be on a stage or at the front of a class.

Make an effort to get closer to your audience no matter where you're standing and speaking. Consider the relationship between your topic and where you are in your performance space. Can the topic you're discussing be connected to your stage position? How can you move around your space in a dramatic way that emphasizes points and gets your information across in an engaging, captivating way?

How about the way that you sound? This is something paramount to the theatre experience as well as public speaking. When you study theatre and acting, you will see that capturing, maintaining, and using your voice like a tool is vital and one of the first things a performer learns about. If you want to communicate the nuanced implications of your remarks, you need to think about how you sound and how your voice exits your body and travels to observers. Too many speakers don't understand the value and force of silence. Allow your audience to feel the seriousness and weight of what you're saying. Take pauses, find certain points to hit hard, and fluctuate your volume.

Remember that it doesn't matter how many people are watching you. Just like you would tell a tale to your best buddy, you can also tell it to hundreds of other people.

When first study acting, you are taught how to "find your light." This is a practice that every actor is familiar with. It implies that if you're on stage and it's dark, go to the spotlight or section of the stage that is visible so that people can see you. It makes perfect sense. This is all about drawing attention to yourself and hooking them with everything you do. Why should they pay attention? Why should they follow you around the stage to see what you do next? This is something that both the stage performer and public speaker need to keep in mind during a show.

And always let your personality shine. This is something that the best stage performers know. They know you need to engage your audience; your persona needs to draw them in. Something about you attracts them to every word you say. Is charisma a mystical, ethereal factor you possess? Can you gain charisma and relay it by smiling subtly? Yes. Simply said, charisma is the ability to be oneself while attracting the attention of others.

When you speak in front of an audience, building a relationship with them is important. It's a connection founded on communication, information sharing, and respect. In a performance, both you and the viewers have a role to play. It's the job of the actor (public speaker) to give the audience a reason to watch and pay attention.

Yes, you can learn an awful lot about public speaking by following some of the basic principles you'll pick up in theatre class. You don't have to be an Oscar winner either; just a little bit of theatre will take you to the next level.

HOW TO AUDITION

Arriving at an audition ten minutes early will show your interest and dependability. Treat the audition like a job interview. Avoid acting inappropriately (e.g., chewing gum, engaging in aimless chatter with stage workers), or giving extensive monologues about why you're the ideal candidate for the position.

Typically, business casual dress is recommended. Although you don't want to look like a stockbroker or banker, you nevertheless want to project a serious attitude. Keep in mind that many aspiring actors make the mistake of overdressing for auditions.

If you are required to do a monologue for your audition, be sure you have thoroughly practiced it. Understand the character and scene entirely rather than merely memorizing the phrases without comprehension. This is when you leave the greatest impact on the people running the show. Wow the director as they notice the stark contrast between the person who just greeted them and the person who is now taking shape on stage. Show your range and how much effort you've put into the audition.

A stage performer is typically their harshest critic following an audition. Try to avoid this, and don't get stuck in your head. Simply thank the theatrical director and promptly exit the stage.

CHAPTER NINE:

EXERCISES TO BRUSH UP ON YOUR PUBLIC SPEAKING SKILLS

TIMED SPEECHES

If you're looking to improve and feel more comfortable giving speeches, put some pressure on yourself. Not too much pressure, of course; that will only result in anxiety. But you should certainly push yourself to see how much more you can improve your skills

Timed speeches are a great way to do just that. You take your subject and set a time limit while trying to squeeze every word into that limit. In doing so, you push yourself to relay all the information in a short amount of time.

Don't make the time limit too short, but don't give yourself too much time either. This will help you speak quickly, confidently, and with knowledge and emotion.

INFOMERCIAL EXERCISE

Here's a good challenge: Sell your friend something. Not a car or the latest and greatest phone. Instead, sell them the coffee cup sitting next to you or the shoes on your feet. This is the basis for the infomercial exercise you can practice as you brush up on your public speaking skills.

The exercise is simple: Take an object in your home and pitch it like a great salesperson. You should try to do this with charisma and energy. Creating a good sales pitch requires confidence, projection, human connection, and speaking with authority.

The object you're selling doesn't matter. This is a great test of taking everything you've learned about public speaking and putting it all together.

WRITING A SPEECH ON YOUR FAVORITE MOVIE

Speeches are always better when they focus on things people are passionate about. What makes you more passionate than your favorite movie?

Write a short speech about your favorite film. What makes it the best? Why do you love it so much? What makes it so perfect? How do you convince other people to watch it? These are a few things to keep in mind when you start writing. You'll be pleasantly surprised by how easily the words pour out of you. It will be totally natural because it's something you know that makes you happy. Let your passion write the speech.

To make this exercise even more challenging, give yourself a time limit that will make you get the point across succinctly with passion and energy. Then strive to maintain the same energy and passion in every speech you give, even if it's not about something you love.

If you don't want to write about your favorite movie, write a speech about your favorite month, birthday, or vacation. Anything you love can be used with this technique.

PRACTICE DEBATING
THE OPPOSITE SIDE
OF YOUR OPINION

We've mentioned before that you should know both sides of any debate you're a part of. Debating the opposite side will not only open your worldview more, but you'll also feel more comfortable talking about things once you've done your research. It can be a challenge, but it will certainly help, and you'll learn something new as well.

CHAPTER TEN:

USING THESE SKILLS AS YOU GROW UP

Public speaking skills will help you in many ways, including getting a job. Many businesses want to hire people who are socially comfortable and able to understand others and convey their thoughts clearly. These are universal skills that you will use throughout your life.

When you look for a job, let the whole world know what you're capable of! Let them know you can talk to anyone about anything. From customers to fellow workers, you will be able to confidently get any point across.

A good public speaker is also a good employee. You might not think that public speaking is something that you should put in your resume or a job application, but it's an important piece of information. This is the sort of skill that employers look for.

USING QUICK THINKING SKILLS IN INTERVIEWS

Your training in public speaking will help you when you interview for that position you really want. Think about it: Public speaking is about selling facts, emotions, and opinions. You convey these things to make people believe them.

Pitching yourself to a prospective employer uses the same skills you picked up when you learned how to give a speech. Speak with enthusiasm and confidence, and you will get your points across and position yourself as the best person for the job.

USING YOUR SKILLS
TO NEGOTIATE
CONTRACTS AND PAY

Again, you're simply selling yourself when you look for a new job. When you want a better contract or a higher rate of pay, you're doing the very same thing.

If you can wow the powers that be with your pitch, you stand a good chance of nailing the interview. Present a short little speech for yourself. Talk about your qualifications for the contract or pay bump— list them out like you would if you were giving a speech. Don't go overboard or sell yourself too hard. Know your audience, and focus on the best ways to create a person-to-person connection.

CONCLUSION

Public speaking doesn't have to be scary. You have many things going on in your life, so it's understandable that public speaking might not be on your radar of the most important talents to have. In fact, you might not ever think about public speaking until your teacher tells you about an upcoming assignment that will require you to step in front of the class and talk to everyone about a subject you're not especially familiar with or fond of.

The good news is that it doesn't matter what you're supposed to speak about. When you're trained in public speaking, you'll be able to nail it no matter what.

Learning about public speaking will do much more for you beyond getting a good grade. It will make you feel better about yourself and give you stronger social skills.

Public speaking isn't about standing in front of people and giving out information. It's about forming a connection with the audience, believing in yourself, and having natural ease in social situations. When you study public speaking, you'll find it's something that can improve your life in many ways.

Regardless of your age or your experience, public speaking can open so many new avenues and opportunities. You'll shine brighter than ever before and feel better about yourself, too. Public speaking is a key to happiness, confidence, and prosperity.

Made in United States
North Haven, CT
05 February 2023